# LEARNING CENTERS
# FOR CHRISTIAN KIDS

by Mary J. Kurth

Cover Illustrated by Laurie Jordan

Illustrated by Susan Hendron

Cover Production by Nehmen-Kodner

All rights reserved—Printed in the U.S.A.
Copyright © 2000 Grace Publications
A Division of Frank Schaffer Publications, Inc.
23740 Hawthorne Blvd., Torrance, CA 90505

Unless otherwise indicated, the New International Version of the Bible was used in preparing the activities in this book. Scripture taken from the HOLY BIBLE, NEW INTERNATIONAL VERSION. Copyright © 1973, 1978, 1984 International Bible Society. Used by permission of Zondervan Bible Publishers.

# Introduction

*Learning Centers for Christian Kids* is a dynamic teaching resource for Christian educators of young children. This Scripture-based resource guide offers you a wonderful variety of hands-on activities and ideas that can be done in centers and that will complement and enhance your current Christian education curriculum. Children will have a marvelous time practicing valuable skills as they learn about God's love for them at the same time.

Each of the eight chapters in this book contains ideas and suggestions for setting up a theme-based learning center filled with exciting activities based on Christian ideals. The centers have been designed to allow children to interact with each other using the materials and activities provided. The materials required are inexpensive, readily available, and familiar to young children, thus making each Scripture-based learning experience concrete and meaningful.

Each chapter includes the following components:

- **Pages 1 and 2—Teacher Resource Pages**—These pages contain a key Bible verse and other related Bible verses/passages, a word list, directions for setting up the center and a list of things to include in it, sentence starters, enrichment and extension activities, and a suggested prayer. (Note: These page numbers also refer to the numbered pages in the chapter. Each chapter is individually numbered from 1–9, and these numbers appear in the top right corner on each page.)

- **Page 3—reproducible Activity Page**

- **Page 4—a reproducible Emergent Reader**—ready for children to color, cut, fold, and read

- **Page 5—reproducible Activity Cards**—ready to be cut apart, perhaps glued onto construction paper for strength, and posted at the learning center along with the materials required for each activity

- **Pages 6 and 7—reproducible Game Pages**—Once the step-by-step preparation is complete, place this learning game at the center for instant fun.

- **Page 8—reproducible Shape Journal Page**—This page is perfect for young believers to use to creatively draw and write about God's word and the topic of study. (Or, the sentence starters in each chapter are perfect to use on this page as well. Also see the Shape Journal Activity Ideas list on pages 4–5 for more ways to use this page.)

- **Page 9—Bible Verse Poster**—This contains a condensed version of the key Bible verse featured in each chapter and can be colored and displayed at the learning center.

# Introduction continued

## Setting Up a Learning Center

Find a space in your classroom or home where you can display the materials and prepared learning activities found in each chapter. It should be a place in which children have freedom to move and interact with each other. A table, bookshelf, or corner of a room works best.

Be sure to have a bulletin board or a clothesline nearby that can be used to display related pictures, the Bible verse posters, or any artwork the children create.

After you choose one of the center topics in this book, search your home or classroom for any objects or artifacts pertaining to the topic that you could put in the center. (Specific ideas for enhancing each learning center environment can be found on the first page in each chapter.) Prepare the reproducible learning games and activities presented in the chapter and attractively display the materials at the center. (For example, post the four Activity Cards at the center along with the required materials; set a stack of the reproducible Emergent Readers, the Activity Page, the Shape Journal Page, the Bible Verse Poster, and crayons and markers at the center. You might also want to include a colored and laminated copy of the Bible Verse Poster in the center.)

On page 6 are eight bookmarks, one relating to each chapter. Use these to mark the featured Bible verse from each chapter in a large Bible so that the children can easily look up the verse.

Page 7 contains a Learning Center Evaluation form. It contains several open-ended statements the children can dictate answers to and a box the children can draw a picture in. Guide the children in drawing a picture of something they learned, an activity they enjoyed, etc. Let them tell you about it to see what they learned or enjoyed in the center. This form is a great way to help motivate the children and to help them recognize skills they might need more practice with. It can also be sent home to parents to inform them of their child's progress.

A letter to parents can be found on page 8. This is good to use to keep parents informed of what their children are doing and to get or keep them involved. Send a copy of this letter home with each child before beginning a new center.

# Introduction continued

## *Ways to Use the Shape Journal Pages*

### Certificates/Awards
Print a positive affirmation in the center of the Shape Journal Page. Use it as an award or certificate of merit for achievement or for positive reinforcement. Suggestions: You Are Special! Great Job! What a Hard Worker!

### Birthday Cards
Write a birthday message in the center of a Shape Journal Page. Have each child in the class sign his or her name. Give the card to the birthday child.

### Word Cards
Each chapter contains a list of words relating to it. Print these words on a Shape Journal Page. Reproduce it and send home a copy with each child. Or, create word cards by printing each word from the chapter Word List on one of the Shape Journal Pages. Post the word cards at the learning center. Set a fun pointer nearby (for example, a closed umbrella for the weather unit). Children will enjoy pointing to each word card and reading it aloud.

### Individual Booklets
Staple several Shape Journal Pages into a booklet for each child. Stack the booklets at the learning center. Invite the children to write and/or draw their responses to the various learning center activities they participate in.

### Language Experience Stories
After a class trip or special class activity, let the children dictate their experiences to you. Print the children's responses on a large sheet of chart paper. Then help each child print his or her own experience onto a Shape Journal Page. Let the children take them home to share.

### Puzzle Page
Draw several lines on a Shape Journal Page to create a puzzle. Make a copy for each child. Have the children draw a picture on their pages and then cut them apart. The children can store their pieces in an envelope and put their puzzles back together.

# Introduction continued

## *Ways to Use the Shape Journal Pages continued*

### Collage Creation Activities
Provide each child with a Shape Journal Page, scissors, glue, and a magazine. Have the children cut out pictures relating to the center's topic from the magazine and glue them onto the page.

### Math Work Mats
Color several Shape Journal Pages, mount them on tagboard, and laminate them. Set these "math mats" in a shoebox along with a set of related manipulatives. Invite the children to count, sort, form patterns with, or add sets of manipulatives on their math mats.

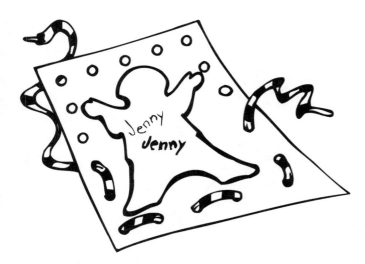

### Sewing Cards
Color several shape journal pages, mount them on tagboard, and laminate them. Punch holes around the edge of each page. Tie a length of string to each card. Place the sewing cards in a basket and set it at the learning center. Children will enhance fine motor skills as they enjoy lacing the cards.

### Name Writing
Provide each child with a Shape Journal Page and three or four colors of markers. Encourage the children to practice writing their names on the pages using the different markers.

### Assessment Tools
Print the alphabet, numbers, shapes, color words, etc., onto a Shape Journal Page. Make copies and use the page to assess learning. Circle the letters, numbers, etc., that the children still need to practice and send the pages home with them.

# Bookmarks

Then God said, "Let the land produce vegetation: seed-bearing plants and trees on the land that bear fruit with seed in it, according to their various kinds." . . . (Genesis 1:11)

Cleanse me with hyssop, and I will be clean; wash me, and I will be whiter than snow. (Psalm 51:7)

There is the sea, vast and spacious, teeming with creatures beyond number—living things both large and small. (Psalm 104:25)

I lie down and sleep; I wake again, because the Lord sustains me. (Psalm 3:5)

"Therefore everyone who hears these words of mine and puts them into practice is like a wise man who built his house on the rock." (Matthew 7:24)

I praise you because I am fearfully and wonderfully made . . . (Psalm 139:14)

So whether you eat or drink or whatever you do, do it all for the glory of God. (1 Corinthians 10:31)

. . . "Praise be to the name of God for ever and ever; wisdom and power are his. He changes times and seasons . . ." (Daniel 2:20–21)

Name _____

# Learning Center Evaluation

I learned about _____

_____ .

My favorite activity was _____

_____ .

I want to work harder at _____

_____ .

_____
date

Dear Parents,

We are setting up a new learning center in our classroom. It is entitled _____. This center features this Bible verse: _____

_____

_____

Some other Bible verses/stories relating to the center are these:

_____

_____

Please share and discuss the Bible verses/stories listed above with your child and family. Perhaps you could all memorize one of the verses.

Also, if you have any items relating to the topic that you would like to share, we would appreciate them greatly.

Thank you for your interest.

Sincerely,

# Seasons and Weather

. . . *"Praise be to the name of God for ever and ever; wisdom and power are his. He changes times and seasons . . ."* (Daniel 2:20–21)

Young believers will be fascinated with God's sovereign control over the seasons and weather as they participate in the activities found in this learning center.

### More From the Bible About the Seasons and Weather
Genesis 6–8 (the flood), Psalm 77:17–18, Psalm 147:15–18, Psalm 148:7–8

## Things to Include at the Center

- copies of Activity Pages 3–4
- Activity Cards (page 5) and any materials needed to complete the activities
- prepared Weather Lotto Game (pages 6–7)
- copies of the Shape Journal Page (page 8)
- copies of the Bible Verse Poster (page 9); include one on display
- assortment of art supplies
- children's literature selections relating to seasons and weather
- assortment of pictures and photographs relating to seasons and weather
- seasonal clothing articles for children to try on
- seasonal objects and artifacts

## Word List
Print the following vocabulary words on 3" x 5" note cards and post them around the center: *snow, wind, rain, sun, clouds, hail, cold, hot, warm, scarf, hat, mittens, glove, jacket, umbrella.* Children can refer to the word cards when writing or reading at the center.

## Directions

1. Discuss the key Bible verse featured above (and the condensed version on the poster page).

2. Go over each activity on pages 3–9 with the children. Demonstrate how to complete each activity from start to finish.

3. Invite the children to explore with the materials at the center and discuss their findings with each other.

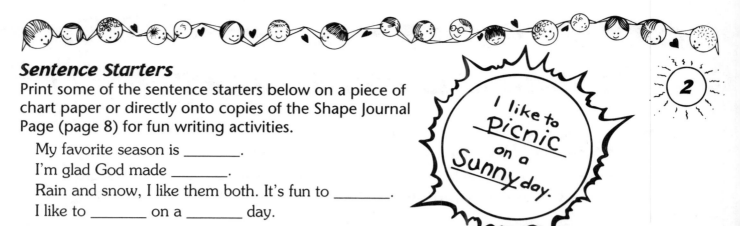

## Sentence Starters

Print some of the sentence starters below on a piece of chart paper or directly onto copies of the Shape Journal Page (page 8) for fun writing activities.

My favorite season is _____.

I'm glad God made _____.

Rain and snow, I like them both. It's fun to _____.

I like to _____ on a _____ day.

## For More Fun

Hang several colorful umbrellas from the ceiling above the learning center. Suspend a paper sun, raindrops, and clouds from the ceiling as well. Place a fan at the center.

## Enrichment Activities

### Seasonal Sorting and Graphing

Place a large assortment of seasonal clothing articles and objects in a laundry basket. Place four seasonal picture cards, one per season, in the basket. Invite small groups of children to lay the picture cards in a row across the floor. Then have the children sort the items into the corresponding columns. Have the children discuss the information from the graph using questions similar to these: *How many items were in each row? Which column had the most items? the fewest?* etc.

| sunny | cloudy | rainy | snowy | foggy | windy |
|---|---|---|---|---|---|
| | | | | | |
| | | | | | |
| | | | | | |
| | | | | | |

### Daily Weather Graph

On a large sheet of posterboard, make six columns. Draw a weather symbol at the top of each column and write one of the following words: *sunny, cloudy, rainy, snowy, foggy, windy.* Divide each column into 20 or so squares. Each day, invite children to assess the daily weather. After determining the weather, let a child color in the appropriate square. Do this for each month.

### Choral Reading Presentation

Divide the children into small groups. Assign each group one of the following Bible verses to memorize and recite: Daniel 2:21; Psalm 148:7; Psalm 147:8, 16, 17, 18. Have each group make an illustrated poster or mural to correspond with its verse. Have the children do a short presentation to another class or to the congregation, reciting their assigned verses and showing their artwork. Have the entire class memorize the text to the Emergent Reader on page 4 and recite it at the end of the presentation.

### Suggested Prayer

Dear God, thank you so much for creating the different seasons and all the different types of weather. Great are you Lord and mighty in power. Some of us like snow best. Some of us like sunny days best. We appreciate you giving us so much beauty to enjoy in this world. Amen.

## Activity Page

Color the pictures. Draw yourself on each page. Cut out the boxes on the solid lines. Paste the boxes end to end to make a long strip. Fold on the dotted lines to make the strip stand up.

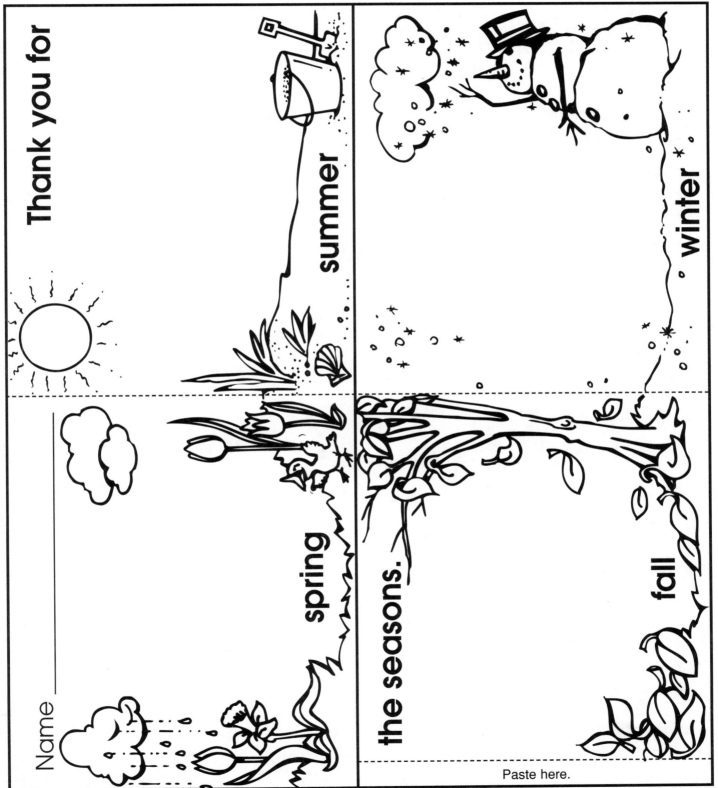

Thank you for

summer

winter

Name _____

spring

the seasons.

fall

Paste here.

3

*He spreads the snow like wool . . . (Psalm 147:16)*

*Great is our Lord and mighty in power . . . (Psalm 147:5)*

2

*. . . he supplies the earth with rain . . . (Psalm 147:8)*

*Great is our Lord and mighty in power . . . (Psalm 147:5)*

*. . . he stirs up his breezes . . . (Psalm 147:18)*

*Great is our Lord and mighty in power . . . (Psalm 147:5)*

4

# Great Is Our Lord

*He covers the sky with clouds . . . (Psalm 147:8)*

*Great is our Lord and mighty in power . . . (Psalm 147:5)*

**Activity Cards**
Cut apart the cards. Glue them to construction paper. Put them at the center along with any necessary materials.

5

## Cut and Paste a Sun
**Materials Needed:**
blue and yellow construction paper, scissors, glue

### Directions:
1. Cut a round sun from the yellow paper.
2. Glue it onto the blue paper.
3. Cut sun rays from the yellow scraps of paper.
4. Glue them around the sun.
5. Hang your picture at the learning center.

## Counting Clouds
**Materials Needed:**
one die, cotton balls (clouds), one blue sheet of construction paper folded into four sections

### Directions:
1. Roll the die.
2. Count out the number of "clouds" and place them in the first section on the paper.
3. Repeat the activity for the other three sections.
4. Count how many "clouds" you have altogether.
5. Clear the sections and play again.

## Seasonal Clothing
**Materials Needed:**
an assortment of seasonal clothing items: winter hat, scarf, mittens, boots, jacket, snow pants, raincoat, umbrella, etc.

### Directions:
1. Over your clothes, try on some clothing for a certain kind of weather.
2. Have someone guess which kind of weather you are dressed for.
3. Repeat the activity using clothing for a different kind of weather.

## Raindrop Art
**Materials Needed:**
paper, crayons, eyedropper, 1 cup blue water wash (1 cup water, 1 T. blue paint)

### Directions:
1. Draw a picture of yourself holding an umbrella.
2. Use the eyedropper and blue water wash to make raindrops on the page.
3. Let the page dry and hang it up at the center.

## Game

Color this page and page 7. Glue each page to tagboard and laminate. Cut apart the two lotto game cards (page 7) and the letter cards (below). Place the materials in a resealable bag with the directions card (below). Invite pairs of children to play Weather Lotto.

### Weather Lotto
**Directions:**

1. Each player takes a lotto card.
2. Stack the letters facedown on the table.
3. Turn over the letter on the top of the stack.
4. Name the letter and the type of weather picture.
5. The person who has the matching letter/picture places the letter on his or her lotto card.
6. Take turns drawing letters until both lotto cards are full.

God changes seasons. (Daniel 2:21)

9

# Eat and Drink

*So whether you eat or drink or whatever you do, do it all for the glory of God.* (1 Corinthians 10:31)

Young children will enjoy actively participating in these activities relating to food and drink as they learn more about God's word.

### More From the Bible About Eating and Drinking
Matthew 6:25–34 (Do Not Worry), Deuteronomy 6:11, Genesis 2:5–3:13 (Adam and Eve in the Garden), 1 Corinthians 11:23–26 (The Last Supper), Matthew 14:13–21 (Jesus Feeds the Five Thousand)

## Things to Include at the Center
- copies of Activity Pages 3–4
- Activity Cards (page 5) and any materials needed to complete the activities
- prepared A Is for Apple Card Game (pages 6–7)
- copies of the Shape Journal Page (page 8)
- copies of the Bible Verse Poster (page 9); include one on display
- assortment of art supplies
- children's literature selections relating to food and drink
- collection of empty food containers, plastic or toy foods, dry or canned foods
- collection of various paper or plastic plates, silverware, cups, napkins, etc. (birthday party or holiday assortments provide color and fun)
- picnic basket containing tablecloth and food or table service items
- variety of plastic jars containing dry food items for counting
- menus or place mats from various restaurants
- assorted cooking and baking equipment and utensils

### Word List
Print the following vocabulary words on 3" x 5" note cards and post them around the center: *eat, drink, chew, swallow, breakfast, lunch, dinner, snack, healthy, energy, strength.* Children can refer to the word cards when writing or reading at the center.

### Directions
1. Discuss the key Bible verse featured above (and the condensed version on the poster page).
2. Go over each activity on pages 3–9 with the children. Demonstrate how to complete each activity from start to finish.
3. Invite the children to explore with the materials at the center and discuss their findings with each other.

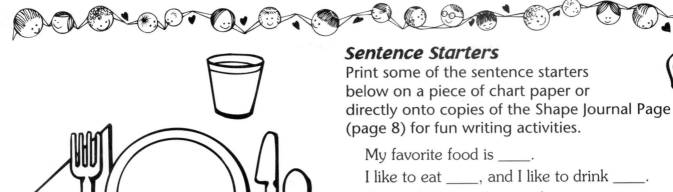

## Sentence Starters

Print some of the sentence starters below on a piece of chart paper or directly onto copies of the Shape Journal Page (page 8) for fun writing activities.

My favorite food is ____.

I like to eat ____, and I like to drink ____.

I'm glad God made ____ for us to eat.

I'm thankful for ____ because ____.

____ gives me energy and helps me to grow.

Today, I will eat ____.

### For More Fun

Bring in a child's kitchen set (stove, sink, refrigerator), aprons, chef's hat, notepad and pencil, menus, toy cash register, and money. Invite the children to take turns role-playing a "restaurant" scene involving a cook, a waitress, customers, and a cashier.

## Enrichment Activities

### Field Trip/Resource Person

Visit a local grocery store or restaurant. After touring the business, have the children draw and write about the learning experience. If a field trip isn't possible, invite a resource person, such as a cook, chef, waitress, or grocer, to come to the classroom and tell about his or her job and share his or her faith with the children.

### Friendship Feast

Set aside one day as "Friendship Feast Day." Invite each child to bring in a favorite prepared food or beverage item to share with the class. (Have parent volunteers help prepare the table and food items.) Encourage the children to share a word of thanksgiving with the class and then eat together and celebrate God's goodness in blessing us with friends, family, and food.

You may want to simplify the feast by having a theme food such as salad (everyone brings in a salad topping), trail mix (everyone brings in one cup of cereal or other small edibles), or vegetables and fruit (everyone brings in a prepared vegetable and/or cut-up fruit for fruit salad).

### Food/Word Matching Game

Have each child hold an empty food container from the learning center. Print a word card to match each food item. Have the children sit in a circle. Stack the word cards facedown in the center of the circle. Turn over the top word card and read it aloud. The child holding that food sets his or her food down and reads the word aloud. The entire class recites aloud "Thank you, God, for giving us ____," adding in the name of the food item. The game continues until all the cards have been read and the children have thanked God for each type of food.

### Suggested Prayer

Dear God, thank you for making food and drinks for us to enjoy. Thank you for the food that makes us strong and gives us energy. Help us to remember you whenever we eat and drink. Amen.

Name _____

# Have a Picnic

Roll a die. Write the number next to one of the foods below. Draw that number and kind of food on the blanket. Do this for each food. Color.

3

God gives us all
kinds of food . . .

2

God gives us food
that is sweet.

. . .for you and
me to eat.

4

# God Gives
# Us Food

God gives us food
that is salty.

## Activity Cards

Cut apart the cards. Glue them to construction paper. Put them at the center along with any necessary materials.

### Sort and Graph
**Materials Needed:**
food and drink containers and related objects; word cards containing these words: *eat, drink*

**Directions:**
1. Sort the objects into two piles: *eat* and *drink.*
2. Lay each pile of objects in a row across the floor.
3. Label each row with a word card.
4. Count how many objects are in each row.

### Food and Drink Collage
**Materials Needed:**
large sheet of mural paper, magazines, glue, scissors

**Directions:**
1. Look through the magazines for pictures of food and drink.
2. Cut out the pictures.
3. Glue them onto the mural paper in collage formation.
4. Throw your scraps in the trash.

### Count How Many
**Materials Needed:**
three or more clear plastic containers of dry foods, such as cereal, pasta, crackers, etc.

**Directions:**
1. Choose a container.
2. Carefully spill out the contents.
3. Count how many pieces are in the container.
4. Put the pieces back in.
5. Repeat the activity for the other containers.

### Set the Table
**Materials Needed:**
one die; large assortment of tableware: plates, cups, silverware, napkins

**Directions:**
1. Roll the die and say the number.
2. Set the table for that many people.
3. Clear the table and repeat the activity.

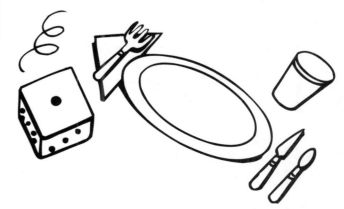

## Game

Make a copy of this page and page 7. Glue each page to tagboard. Color each picture. Cut apart the cards. Punch a hole beneath each letter. On the back of each card, write the letter with the same beginning sound as the food shown. Place the cards and two pencils in a resealable bag along with the directions card below.

### A Is for Apple

**Directions:**

1. Choose a card.

2. Name the food.

3. Look at the letters on the card. Which letter does the food start with?

4. Poke the pencil through the hole with the same beginning sound.

5. Look at the back of the card to see if you are right.

6. Do the same with the other cards.

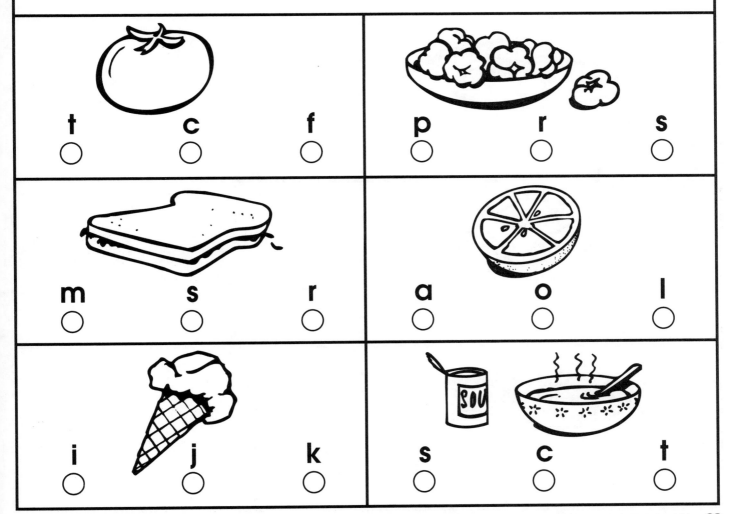

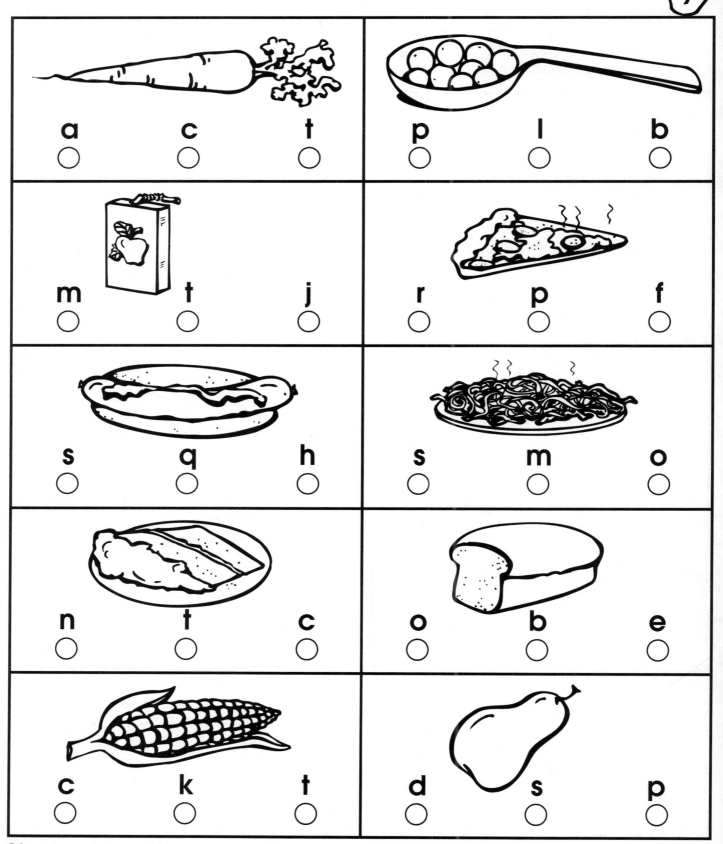

a ○    c ○    t ○

p ○    l ○    b ○

m ○    t ○    j ○

r ○    p ○    f ○

s ○    q ○    h ○

s ○    m ○    o ○

n ○    t ○    c ○

o ○    b ○    e ○

c ○    k ○    t ○

d ○    s ○    p ○

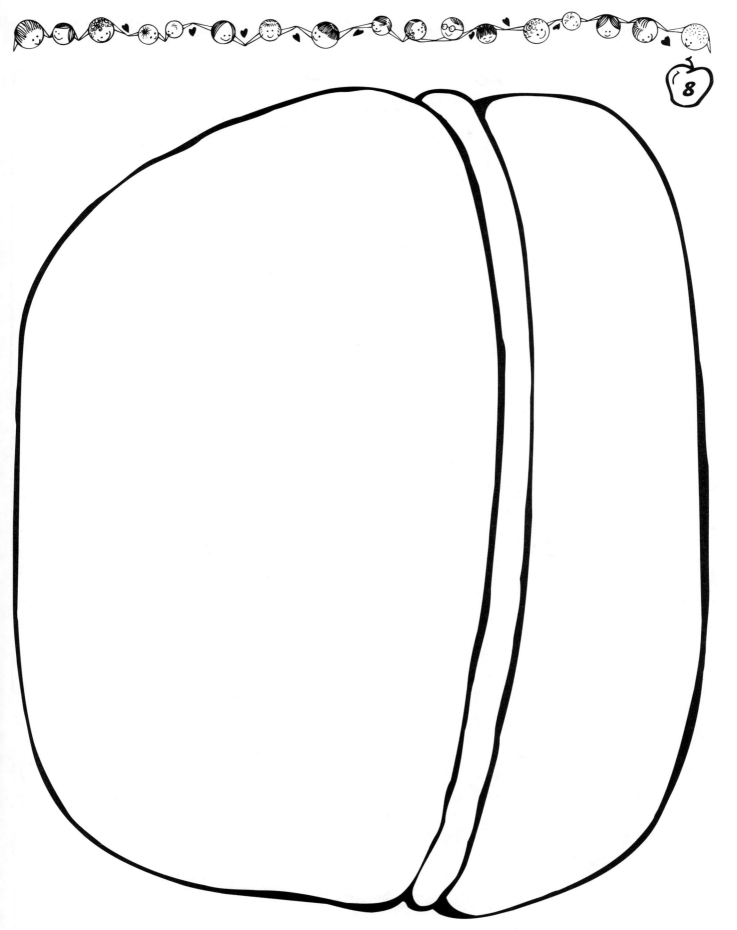

# Be a Builder

*"Therefore everyone who hears these words of mine and puts them into practice is like a wise man who built his house on the rock."* (Matthew 7:24)

Children will enjoy learning about God's word and how to be builders as they participate in these Scripture-based learning center activities.

### More From the Bible About Building
Matthew 7:24–27 (The Wise and Foolish Builders), 1 Kings 6 (Solomon Builds the Temple), 1 Thessalonians 5:11, Psalm 127:1, Ephesians 4:16, Isaiah 57:14, Hebrews 3:4

## Things to Include at the Center
- copies of Activity Pages 3–4
- Activity Cards (page 5) and any materials needed to complete the activities
- prepared Be a Builder Game (pages 6–7)
- copies of the Shape Journal Page (page 8)
- copies of the Bible Verse Poster (page 9); include one on display
- assortment of art supplies
- children's literature selections relating to building
- an assortment of building materials (i.e., wooden blocks, Legos™, Lincoln Logs™, one-inch cubes, etc.)
- assortment of real and toy tools
- hard hat, toolbox, tool belt, children's workbench, safety glasses
- rulers, measuring tape, pencils
- collection of toy working trucks
- tub of wet sand, various sizes of plastic cups or buckets, shovel
- assortment of pictures and photographs of various buildings and homes and of people building them
- piece of wood, large-head nails, hammer

## Word List
Print the following vocabulary words on 3" x 5" note cards and post them around the center: *build, pound, hammer, nails, saw, wood, house, building, rock, sand.* Children can refer to the word cards when writing or reading at the center.

## Directions
1. Discuss the key Bible verse featured above (and the condensed version on the poster).
2. Go over each activity on pages 3–9 with the children. Demonstrate how to complete each activity from start to finish.
3. Invite the children to explore with the materials at the center and discuss their findings with each other.

## Sentence Starters

Print some of the sentence starters below on a piece of chart paper or directly onto copies of the Shape Journal Page (page 8) for fun writing activities.

> If I were a builder, I would _____.
> I can build a _____.
> God built _____.
> I can build others up by _____.

## For More Fun

Stock the center with a large amount of small wood scraps, nails, and hammers. Invite a parent volunteer to supervise this activity. Invite the children to practice building and creating with the materials by nailing small pieces of wood together. Provide paints and paintbrushes so children can add color to their completed projects. (Simply painting wood with water can be great fun as well.)

## Enrichment Activities

### Building Together

Have the children sit in a circle on the floor. Place a large number of wooden blocks and a die in the center of the circle. Have the first child roll the die, count out that number of blocks, and begin to build a building in the center of the circle. As the children take turns rolling the die, they add to the construction of the building. Continue until all children have had a turn and the building is complete. Or, play until the building falls down. For math enrichment, record the number each child rolls. Have the children add up the numbers and then count all the blocks used in the building.

### Wall of Encouragement

Cut a large amount of 6" x 11" bricks from colored construction paper. Print positive phrases on several of the bricks and tack them to the wall. Each time the class gathers together, print a different positive phrase on five or more bricks and add them to the wall. Encourage the children to practice saying the words of encouragement throughout the weeks. Watch as your wall of encouragement grows taller and taller.

### Build Up!

Read Isaiah 57:14 aloud to the class. Print the verse on the chalkboard or chart paper. Lay a section of road (black paper with a segmented line down the middle) on the floor. Call one child forward to stand on the road. Have the class chant this verse aloud in unison: . . . *"Build up, build up, prepare the road! . . ."* (Isaiah 57:14) Encourage the children to think of a positive phrase to say to the child standing before them. Call on several children to verbalize their positive comments (examples: "I like you;" "You're a good friend;" "I'm glad you're in this class;" etc.). Have a different child stand on the road and continue the game. Play until all the children have had a turn at being "built up."

### Suggested Prayer

Heavenly Father, thank you so much for teaching us how to build each other up. Thank you for your word and for showing us how to build our lives on you. You are a great God and a great builder. Amen.

## Activity Page

Cut apart and color the pictures. Fold on the dotted lines. Paste the house together as shown. Set the roof on top of the house. Attach the roof to the house with a small piece of tape.

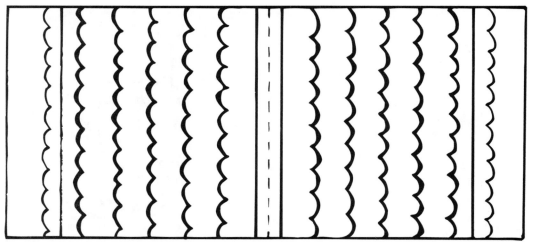

Fold and glue.

Fold and glue.

***Emergent Reader***
Color, cut, fold, and read.

---

**3**

He made the
moon and stars.

God is the builder of
everything.

---

**2**

He made you and me!

God is the builder of
everything.

---

God is the builder
of everything.

He made everything
that is ours.

**4**

---

# God Is the Builder
of Everything

(Hebrews 3:4)

He made the earth
and the sea.

---

## Activity Cards

Cut apart the cards. Glue them to construction paper. Put them at the center along with any necessary materials.

### Build a House

**Materials Needed:**
wooden, plastic, or commercially-prepared building blocks

**Directions:**
1. Build a small building with the blocks.
2. Build a large building with the blocks.
3. Count how many blocks you use as you work.

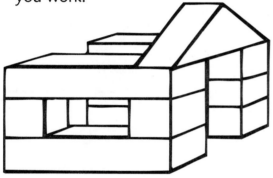

### Use a Hammer

**Materials Needed:**
wooden blocks—each with a number or letter drawn on it with a dotted pencil line, hammer, nails

**Directions:**
1. Choose a piece of wood.
2. Identify the letter or number.
3. Pound nails into the wood to create the letter or number shape.

### Shape Buildings

**Materials Needed:**
an assortment of colored paper shapes, glue, drawing paper, scissors, construction paper scraps, crayons

**Directions:**
1. Use the paper shapes to make two or more buildings on your paper.
2. Glue the shapes to the paper.
3. Cut paper shapes from the scraps to make windows, doors, and chimneys.
4. Glue the windows, doors, and chimneys to the buildings.
5. Add details (sun, trees, birds, etc.) to your picture using crayons.

### Build in Sand

**Materials Needed:**
tub of wet sand, plastic containers in various sizes, shovel, stones, small sticks, toy working trucks

**Directions:**
1. Scoop sand into a container.
2. Pack the sand in with your hand.
3. Turn the container over in the sand to create a building.
4. Lift the container off.
5. Add detail to your building with stones and sticks.
6. Make the working trucks drive and move in the sand.

## Game

Make eight copies of the house workspace on page 7. Color each house a different color or reproduce it onto eight different colors of paper. Prepare a large amount (about 40) of builder manipulatives (below). Glue all materials to tagboard and laminate. Make a set of number cards 1–8. Place the materials along with the directions card in a large envelope or resealable bag. (Optional: Use simple equation cards in place of number cards, and have children count and add sets of builder manipulatives.)

### Be a Builder

**Directions:**

1. Lay the eight houses on the floor.

2. Set a number card near each house.

3. Count out the right number of builders and place them on each house.

4. Say a number sentence to tell how many builders are working on each house. (Example: Six builders are working on the orange house. Two builders are working on the red house.)

5. Show a friend your work. Have a friend try the activity.

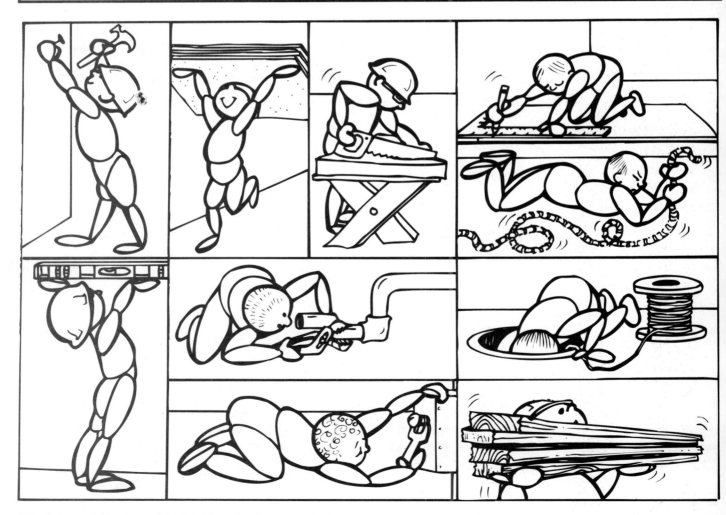

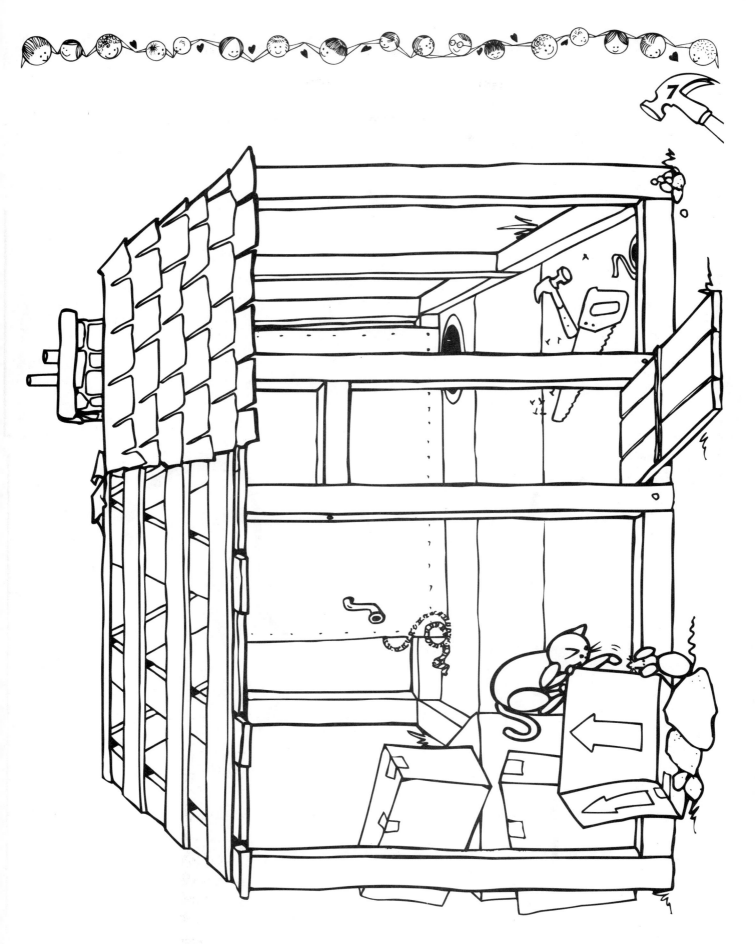

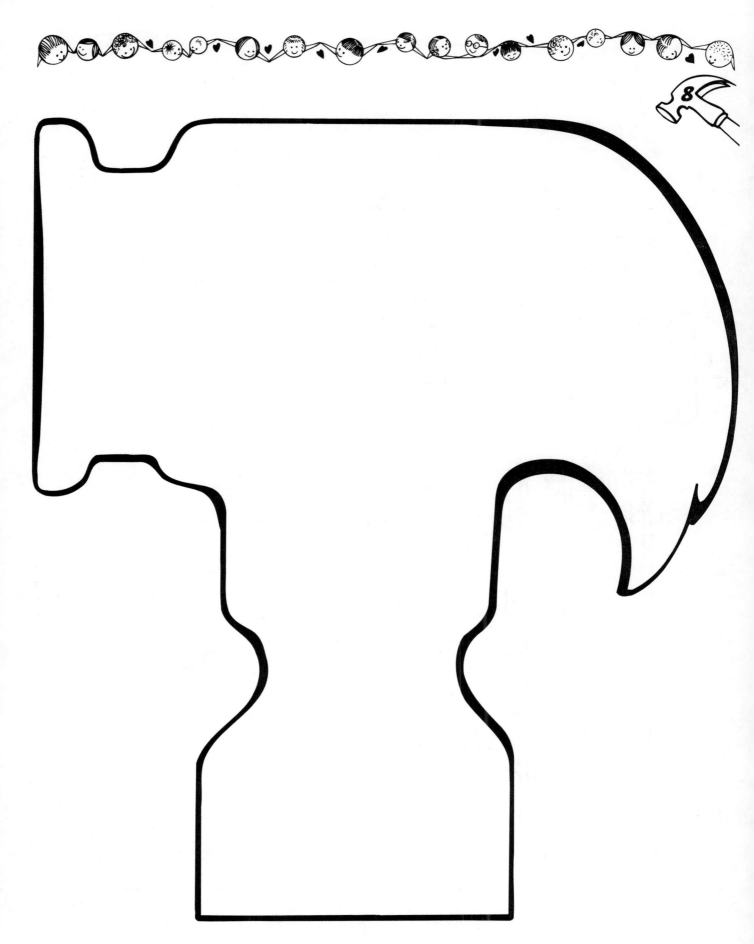

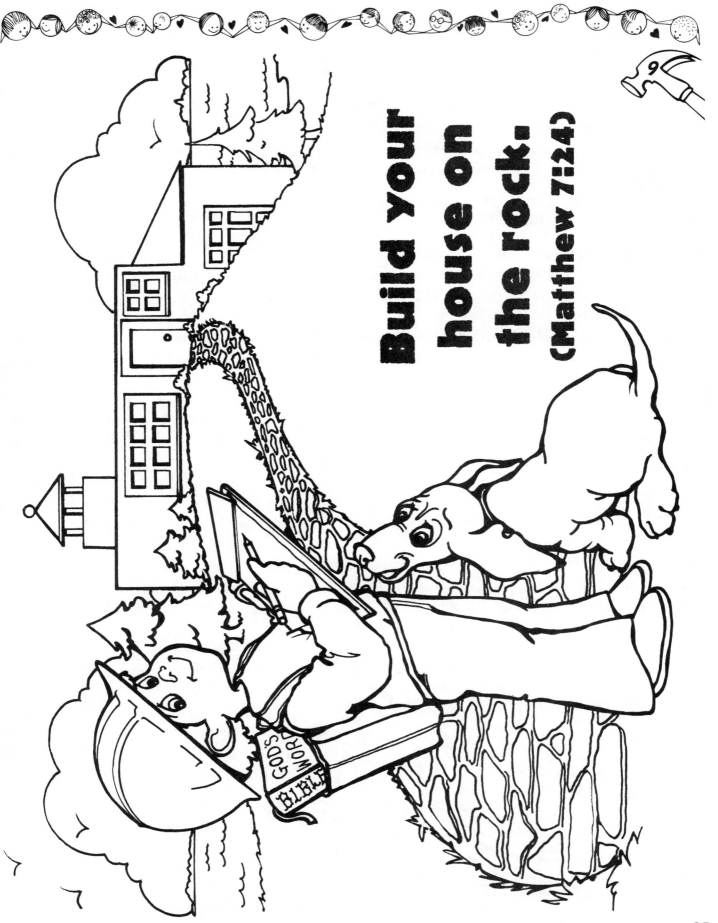

Build your house on the rock. (Matthew 7:24)

# The Sea and All That Is in It

*There is the sea, vast and spacious, teeming with creatures beyond number—living things both large and small.* (Psalm 104:25)

Children will enjoy learning more about God's great creation under the sea as they actively participate in these learning center activities.

### More From the Bible About the Sea
Book of Jonah, Genesis 1:20–23, Psalm 24:1–2

## Things to Include in the Center
- copies of Activity Pages 3–4
- Activity Cards (page 5) and any materials needed to complete the activities
- prepared Sea Life Number Game (pages 6–7)
- copies of the Shape Journal Page (page 8)
- copies of the Bible Verse Poster (page 9); include one on display
- assortment of art supplies
- variety of children's literature selections relating to the sea
- tub of sand, sand shovel, and sand pail
- collection of seashells, starfish, sand dollars, or other sea artifacts
- pictures and photographs of the underwater world
- fishing pole and fishing gear
- fishbowl or aquarium with live fish

## Word List
Print the following vocabulary words on 3" x 5" note cards and post them around the center: *fish, whale, lobster, crab, sea horse, octopus, starfish, water, sand, waves, shark.* Children can refer to the word cards when writing or reading at the center.

## Directions
1. Discuss the Bible verse featured above (and the condensed version on the poster).

2. Go over each activity on pages 3–9 with the children. Demonstrate how to complete each activity from start to finish.

3. Encourage the children to explore with the materials at the center and discuss their findings with each other.

## Sentence Starters

Print some of the sentence starters below on a piece of chart paper or directly on copies of the Shape Journal Page (page 8) for fun writing activities.

God made the ocean. God made the sea.

God made _____ for you and me.

_____ live in the sea.

God made _____ swim in the sea.

In the ocean, you can find a _____.

## For More Fun

Hang a fish net on the ceiling or wall. Display an assortment of ocean artifacts in the net. Lay a colorful air mattress and beach towel on the floor near the center along with some related books and a pair of sunglasses for "seaside" reading pleasure.

## Enrichment Activities

### Field Trip

Take the children on a trip to a local pet store, museum, aquarium, or library to help them learn more about the sea creatures God created.

### Sponge Painting

Provide the children with pre-cut paper fish, shallow pans of paint, and an assortment of sponge pieces. Invite the children to sponge paint patterns and designs on their fish shapes. Hang these at the center.

### Class Mural

Hang a large sheet of blue mural paper on a wall near the center. Invite the children to draw ocean life pictures on the paper. Set a stack of magazines nearby for children to use to cut out pictures to paste on the mural as well.

## Suggested Prayer

Dear God, thank you so much for creating the ocean and all that is in it. You sure did create some interesting and unusual sea creatures. We promise to take care of the ocean and all that lives in it. We love you. It's in your Son's name that we pray. Amen.

# Ocean Graph

Color.

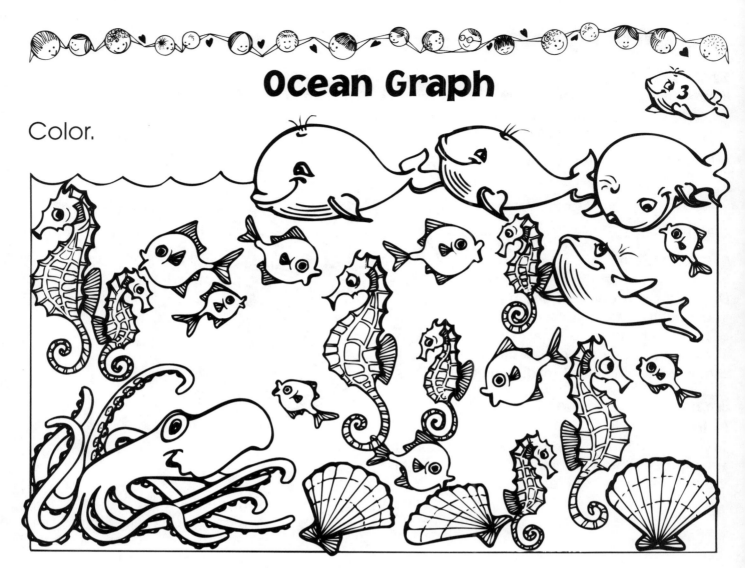

How many? Count and color.

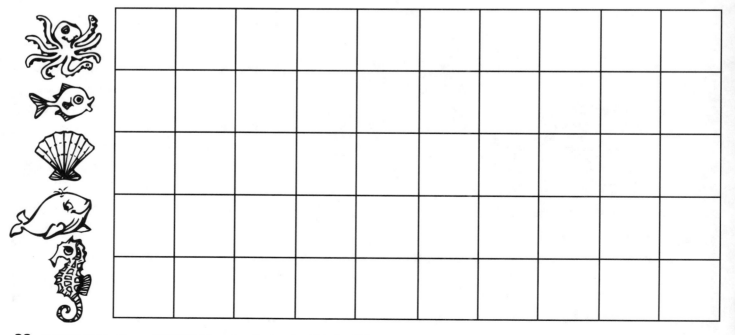

3

God made wind and waves.
The sea is his, for he made it.

2

God made whales and fish.
The sea is his, for he made it.

God made shells and starfish. The sea is his, for he made it.

Thank you, God!

4

The Sea Is His

God made sand and water. The sea is his, for he made it.

# Activity Cards

Cut apart the cards. Glue them to construction paper. Put them at the center along with any necessary materials.

## Swimming in the Sea

**Materials Needed:**
tub of water, tongue depressors (one with each child's name printed on it in permanent marker), orange juice can in which to store tongue depressors

**Directions:**

1. Choose a name stick from the can.

2. Read the name aloud and complete this sentence: "_____ went swimming in the sea."

3. Float the name stick on the water.

4. Repeat steps 1 to 3 until all the names are "swimming in the sea."

## Counting Shells

**Materials Needed:**
two containers of seashells

**Directions:**

1. Spill the shells from one container.

2. Count how many shells are in the pile.

3. Spill the shells from the other container.

4. Guess how many shells are in the pile.

5. Count the shells in the second pile.

## Sandy Shapes

**Materials Needed:**
shapes cut from sandpaper, basket or bag for storage

**Directions:**

1. Choose a partner to work with.

2. Have your partner close his or her eyes.

3. Give the partner a sandpaper shape.

4. Have your partner feel and guess what shape he or she is holding.

5. Take turns and repeat the activity until all the shapes have been guessed.

## Draw the Sea

**Materials Needed:**
crayons, paper, word cards from the learning center

**Directions:**

1. Draw a picture of some sea animals.

2. Look at the word cards. Write some words on your page.

3. Hang your picture at the center.

## Game

Make four copies of each picture card below and on page 7. Mount the picture cards on tagboard. Color and cut them apart. Print a numeral from 1 to 10 on half of the picture cards. Draw sets of 1 to 10 black dots on the rest of the cards. Place the materials in a resealable bag along with the directions card. (To challenge older children, print number words on another set of picture cards and include them in the matching game.)

### Sea Life Number Game

**Directions:**

1. Lay the picture cards out on the floor or table.
2. Pick up a number card.
3. Find the card with the same number of black dots.
4. Lay the pair of cards together.
5. Play until all cards are matched up.

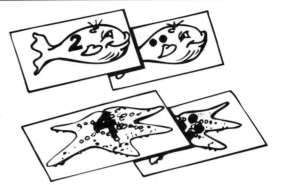

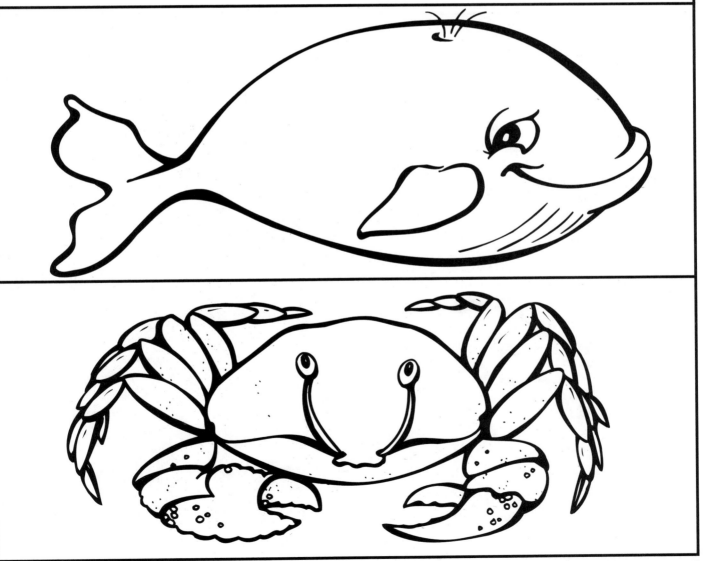

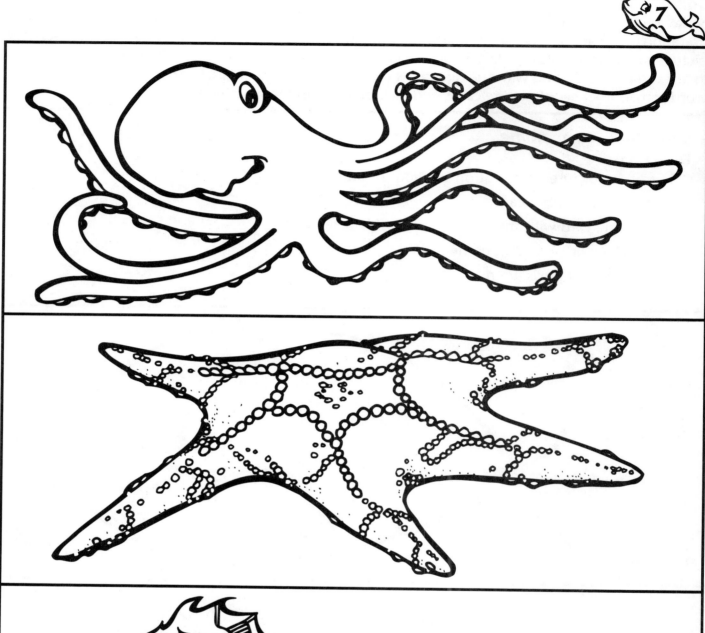

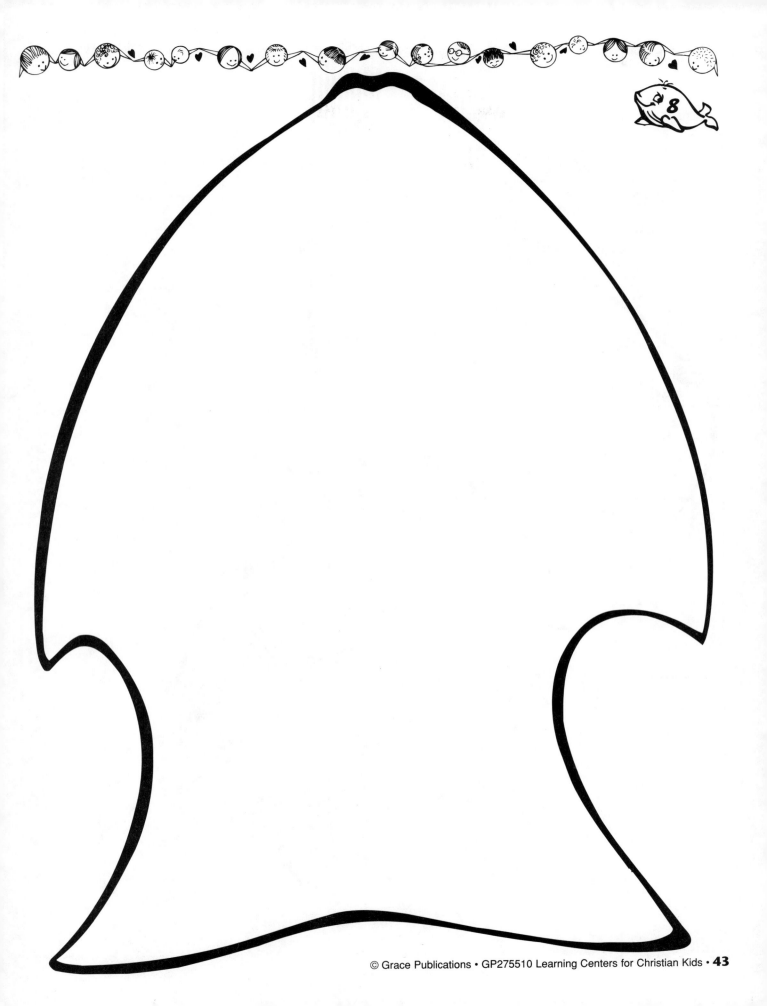

*The sea has many creatures.* (Psalm 104:25)

# Good Night! Sleep and Rest

*I lie down and sleep; I wake again, because the Lord sustains me.*
(Psalm 3:5)

Young believers will enjoy learning what God's word has to say about sleep and rest as they participate in the activities in this learning center.

### More From the Bible About Night, Sleep, and Rest
Proverbs 3:24, Matthew 11:28 (Jesus will give you rest), Genesis 2:21 (Adam sleeps while God creates woman), Psalm 92:1–2

## Things to Include in the Center
- copies of Activity Pages 3–4
- Activity Cards (page 5) and any materials needed to complete the activities
- prepared Good Night A to Z Game on pages 6–7
- copies of the Shape Journal Page (page 8)
- copies of the Bible Verse Poster (page 9); include one on display
- assortment of art supplies
- children's literature selections relating to sleep, rest, nighttime
- pictures or photographs pertaining to nighttime or sleep
- lullaby audiotape and cassette player
- alarm clock—digital and standard
- an assortment of moon and star shapes cut from felt and a flannelboard
- pillows
- teddy bears
- nighttime apparel, including robe, slippers, night cap
- night-light and lamp

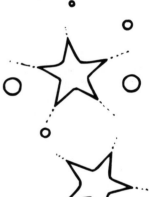

### Word List
Print the following vocabulary words on 3" x 5" note cards and post them around the center: *sleep, rest, night, good night, pillow, bed, blanket, teddy bear, pray, moon, stars, pajamas*. Children can refer to the word cards when writing or reading at the center.

### Directions
1. Discuss the key Bible verse featured above (and the condensed version on the poster page).
2. Go over each activity on pages 3–9 with the children. Demonstrate how to complete each activity from start to finish.
3. Invite the children to explore with the materials at the center and discuss their findings with each other.

## Sentence Starters

Print some of the sentence starters below on a piece of chart paper or directly onto copies of the Shape Journal Page (page 8) for fun writing activities.

At night, I like to _____.
A special place I like to sleep is _____.
Before I go to sleep, I _____.
Bedtime! Bedtime! Time for _____.
At bedtime, our family likes to _____.

## For More Fun

Set a sleeping bag, pillow, flashlight, and a copy of *Good Night, Moon* by Margaret Wise Brown, on the floor near the center. Invite the children to curl up in the sleeping bag and read by the light of the flashlight. (Share this delightful book with the class before placing it at the center.)

## Enrichment Activities

### Pajama Day

Invite the children to bring in or wear pajamas on a designated day. Don't let them forget their teddy bears. Gather the children on the floor, turn the lights down low, let them munch some popcorn, and read aloud the suggested Bible passages about night, sleep, or other bedtime stories.

### Blanket Match

Cut an assortment of "mini blankets" (6" x 6") from fabric scraps. Cut each blanket in half and place all the pieces in a basket. Invite the children to match the patterns on the fabric and then piece the blankets back together.

### Slipper Walk

Make 20 copies of the Shape Journal Page on page 8. (Use bright yellow paper, mount them on tagboard, and laminate them for durability.) Print the numerals 1 to 20 on the moons (one number per moon). Have the children help you lay the trail of moons across the floor in order from 1 to 20. Have one or more children wear a pair of slippers from the learning center and walk along the trail of moons as they name each number.

## Suggested Prayer

Dear God, thank you for watching over us when we sleep. Thank you for placing the moon and the stars in the sky. We pray that you will help us to sleep well, to remember how much you love us, and to praise you as soon as we wake up each morning. Amen.

## Activity Page
Cut out on the dotted lines. Color. Fold on the solid line. Stuff with paper. Staple shut.

**3**

. . . and your faithfulness at night.
(Psalm 92:1-2)

It is good to . . . proclaim
your love in the morning . . .

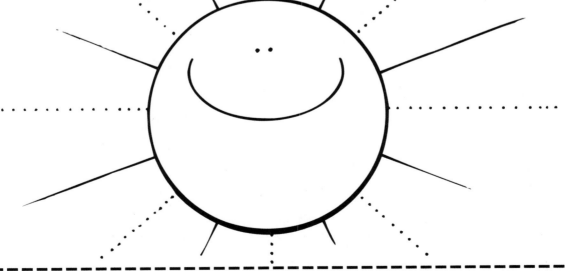

Because you pray and worship God, your sleep will be sweet when you lie down. 3

Because you obey your parents, your sleep will be sweet when you lie down. 2

Because the Lord your God loves you, your sleep will be sweet when you lie down. 4

## Your Sleep Will Be Sweet

(adapted from Proverbs 3:24)

Because you show love to others, your sleep will be sweet when you lie down.

## activity Cards

Cut apart the cards. Glue them to construction paper. Put them at the center along with any necessary materials.

### Patterns in the Sky
**Materials Needed:**
flannelboard, moon and star shapes cut from felt

**Directions:**

1. Make a pattern on the flannelboard using the moon and star shapes.

2. Say the pattern aloud.

3. Make a different pattern on the flannelboard and say it aloud.

4. Show your patterns to a friend.

### Touch and Guess
**Materials Needed:**
pillowcase, a variety of small objects

**Directions:**

1. Place an object inside the pillowcase.

2. Have a friend put his or her hands into the pillowcase and feel the object.

3. Have your friend guess what the object is. Give a hint or two if necessary.

4. Repeat the activity, and take turns as you touch and guess objects.

### Read and Relax
**Materials Needed:**
pillow, books, robe or slippers

**Directions:**

1. Choose a book from the center.

2. Put on the robe or slippers.

3. Relax on a pillow and read.

### Night Words
**Materials Needed:**
plastic or paper letters; word cards depicting these words: *good night, moon, stars, God, sleep*

**Directions:**

1. Stack the word cards facedown.

2. Turn over a card.

3. Read the word(s) aloud.

4. Spell the word(s) using the plastic letters.

5. Repeat the activity until you read and spell each word card.

## Game

Color the game pieces on this page and page 7. Glue the pages to tagboard. Cut apart the pieces and laminate them for durability. Store the pieces in a checkbook box. Invite the children to sequence the alphabet from A to Z.

### Good Night A to Z

**Directions:**

1. Spill out the cards.
2. Lay all the cards faceup.
3. Put the cards in order from A to Z.
4. Show a friend.

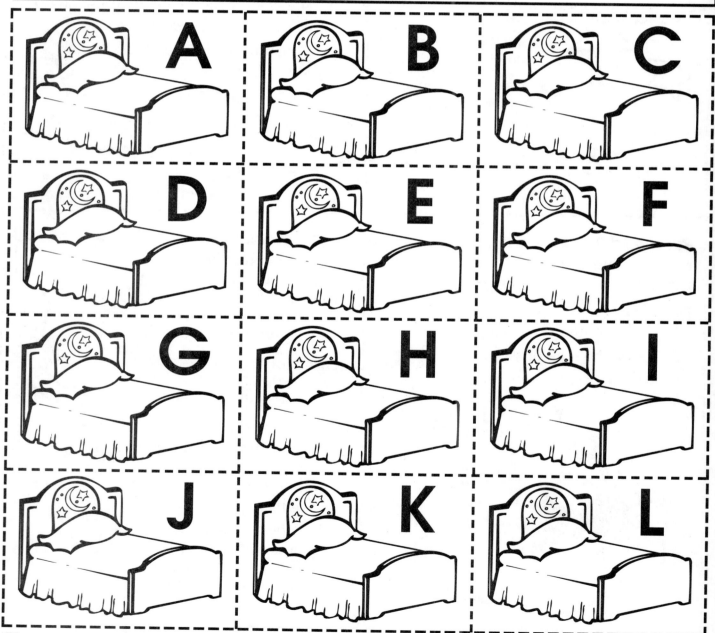

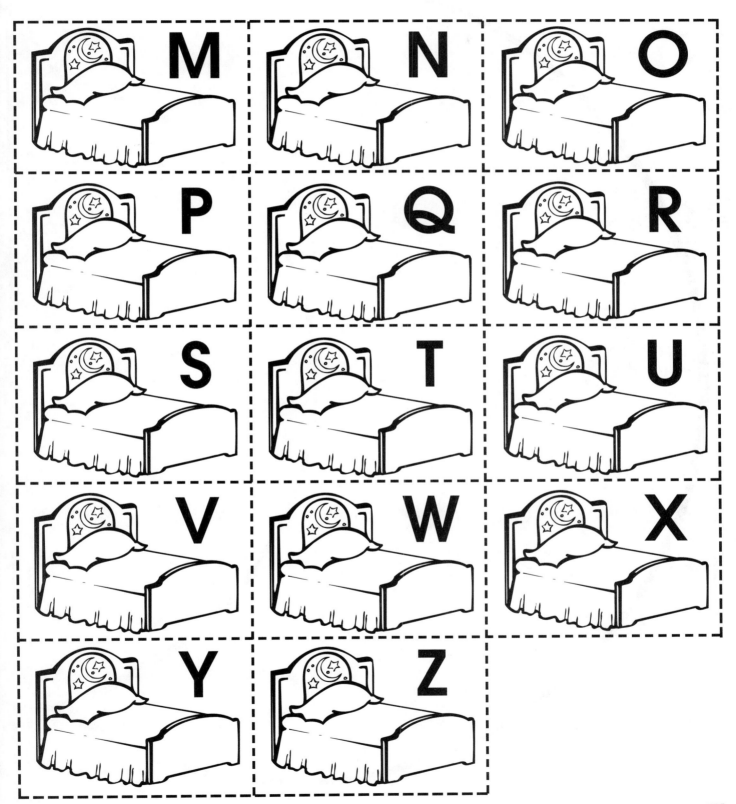

I sleep because the Lord sustains me. (Psalm 3:5)

# Wash Me Clean

*Cleanse me with hyssop, and I will be clean; wash me, and I will be whiter than snow.* (Psalm 51:7)

Children will enjoy learning about being washed clean as they participate in these Scripture-based learning center activities.

### More From the Bible About Washing and Cleansing
John 13:1–17 (Jesus Washes His Disciples' Feet), Luke 5:12 (The Man With Leprosy), Psalm 24:4–5

## Things to Include at the Center
- copies of Activity Pages 3–4
- Activity Cards (page 5) and any materials needed to complete the activities
- prepared Have a Pure Heart Game (pages 6–7)
- copies of the Shape Journal Page (page 8)
- copies of the Bible Verse Poster (page 9); include one on display
- assortment of art supplies
- children's literature selections relating to washing and cleaning
- collection of empty cleaning supply containers: soaps, bubble bath, shampoos, toothpaste, laundry and kitchen soaps
- assortment of bath brushes, sponges, washcloths, cotton swabs, combs, and brushes
- assortment of shapes and colors of bath soaps
- container of baby wipes
- bucket of soapy water and towel
- assortment of pictures and photographs related to cleaning and washing

### Word List
Print the following vocabulary words on 3" x 5" note cards and post them around the center: *wash, clean, bath, water, shower, soap, shampoo, scrub, bubbles.* Children can refer to the word cards when writing or reading at the center.

### Directions
1. Discuss the key Bible verse featured above (and the condensed version on the poster).
2. Go over each activity on pages 3–9 with the children. Demonstrate how to complete each activity from start to finish.
3. Invite the children to explore with the materials at the center and discuss their findings with each other.

## Sentence Starters
Print some of the sentence starters below on a piece of chart paper or directly onto copies of the Shape Journal Page (page 8) for fun writing activities.

We washed _____ in the water.     _____ washed the _____.     The _____ is clean and so am I.
Washing _____ is lots of fun.     A _____ can be whiter than snow.

## For More Fun
Hang a colorful shower curtain as a backdrop in this center. Place a laundry basket of towels and washcloths near the center for the children to fold and sort by size or color.

## Enrichment Activities

### Body Wash
Trace around a child's body on mural paper. Cut out the shape and laminate it. Glue the shape to a piece of cardboard or tagboard for durability. Set a basket of "wipe off" markers or crayons near the body pattern. Invite the children to write or draw on the body and to "wash it clean" with baby wipes or a dry cloth.

### Wash Away My Sin
Provide each child with a small colorful sponge. Recite simple phrases aloud. Then pretend to scrub a specified part of your body with a sponge. Have the children scrub the same part of their bodies as they repeat each phrase after you.

Sample Phrases:
*Wash away my arguing.  (Scrub elbow.)*
*Wash away my anger.  (Scrub knee.)*
*Wash away my lying.  (Scrub face.)*
*Wash away my jealousy.  (Scrub back.)*

### Washing Our Feet
Share John 13:1–17 with the children. Discuss how Jesus washed the feet of his disciples and then asked his disciples to go and do the same. Jesus wanted them to learn to serve each other. Bring in several buckets of soapy water and some towels. Invite the children to take off their shoes and socks and to wash each other's feet as a reminder to serve each other.

### Bathtub Fun
Cut a large bathtub shape from white mural paper. Provide the children with sponges and shallow dishes of pastel paints. Invite small groups of children to sponge paint the tub. When the tub is finished, write out Psalm 51:7 across the front of the tub in large letters. Display this work of art at the center.

### Suggested Prayer
Dear God, thank you for washing us clean by forgiving our sins when we confess them. You are a loving God. Amen.

He who has
clean hands

and a pure
heart, . . .

will receive blessing
from the Lord . . .
(Psalm 24:4–5)

**3**

My father washed the car and . . .

**2**

My mother washed my knee.

# Washed Clean

My sister washed the dishes.

. . . Jesus washed me.

**4**

## Activity Cards

Cut apart the cards. Glue them to construction paper. Put them at the center along with any necessary materials.

### Clean Hands

**Materials Needed:**
bucket of water (or sink), bar of soap, towel, fingernail scrubber

**Directions:**
1. Use soap and water to wash your hands.
2. Scrub your fingernails with the scrubber.
3. Dry your hands on the towel.

### Car Wash

**Materials Needed:**
toothbrush, shallow tray of soapy water, towel, assortment of toy cars

**Directions:**
1. Choose a car to wash.
2. Set it in the tray of water.
3. Use the toothbrush to scrub the car until it's clean.
4. Let the car dry on the towel.

### Number Wash

**Materials Needed:**
shaving cream, table, number formation poster

**Directions:**
1. Squirt a blob of shaving cream (about the size of a golf ball) onto the table.
2. Smooth it out to make a writing surface.
3. Look at the number chart.
4. Write a number in the shaving cream using your index finger.
5. Wipe it away by smoothing the cream over with your hand.
6. Continue writing the numbers 1 to 20.

### Have a Pure Heart

**Materials Needed:**
6-inch red paper heart, pencil, Bible (with Psalm 24:4–5 marked), hole punch, two-foot strands of yarn

**Directions:**
1. Open the Bible to the marked page.
2. Find Psalm 24:4–5 on the page.
3. Write "Psalm 24:4–5" on a paper heart.
4. Punch holes around the edge of the heart and then string it with the yarn.
5. Give the heart to a family member. Ask him or her to look up the verse and read it with you at home.

## Game

Color the game board below and on page 7. Tape the pieces together. Color, cut out, fold and tape the children markers. Glue the board and markers to tagboard. Set the materials and a die in a basket. Invite the children to roll the die and play the game as directed.

### Have a Pure Heart

**Directions:**

1. Place both markers at the starting point of the game.
2. Take turns rolling the die and moving the markers.
3. Complete the directions as stated on the various spaces.
4. When you reach the finish line, you will have achieved a pure heart.

Have a Pure

You have a pure heart!

Say "I'm sorry." Move ahead 1.

Read a Bible verse. Move ahead 2.

Color, cut, fold, and tape.

Heart!

Ask God's forgiveness. Move ahead 2.

Forgive someone. Move ahead 2.

Start

Cleanse me and wash me. (Psalm 51:7)

# Plants and Trees

*Then God said, "Let the land produce vegetation: seed-bearing plants and trees on the land that bear fruit with seed in it, according to their various kinds." . . . (Genesis 1:11)*

Children will enjoy learning more about plants, trees, and God's word as they explore at this hands-on learning center.

### More From the Bible About Plants and Trees
Matthew 13:1–23 (The Parable of the Sower), Matthew 13:24–30 (The Parable of the Weeds)

## Things to Include at the Center
- copies of Activity Pages 3–4
- Activity Cards (page 5) and any materials needed to complete the activities
- prepared Plant and Tree Memory Game (pages 6–7)
- copies of the Shape Journal Page (page 8)
- copies of the Bible Verse Poster (page 9); include one on display
- assortment of art supplies
- children's literature selections relating to plants and trees
- specimens of tree bark, branches, leaves, twigs, vines
- collections of seeds, acorns, nuts, pine cones, seed packets
- a variety of live plants
- an assortment of other products that come from plants and trees
- magnifying glass
- binoculars
- gardening tools and gloves

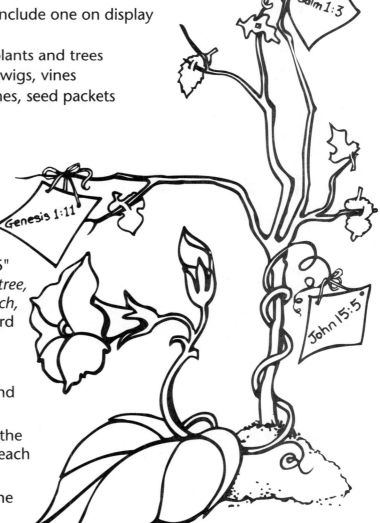

## Word List
Print the following vocabulary words on 3" x 5" note cards and post them around the center: *tree, plant, seed, fruit, root, sun, water, air, leaf, branch, petal, stem, bush.* Children can refer to the word cards when writing or reading at the center.

## Directions
1. Discuss the Bible verse featured above (and the condensed version on the poster).

2. Go over each activity on pages 3–9 with the children. Demonstrate how to complete each activity from start to finish.

3. Encourage the children to explore with the materials at the center and discuss their findings with each other.

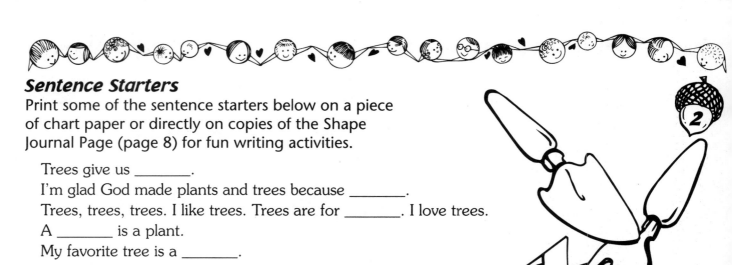

## Sentence Starters
Print some of the sentence starters below on a piece of chart paper or directly on copies of the Shape Journal Page (page 8) for fun writing activities.

Trees give us _____.
I'm glad God made plants and trees because _____.
Trees, trees, trees. I like trees. Trees are for _____. I love trees.
A _____ is a plant.
My favorite tree is a _____.

## For More Fun
Insert a 3–4 foot tree branch into a can of clay or sand. Stand the "tree" near the center. Invite the children to create leaves, insects, animals, etc., from construction paper. Place them in the tree branches.

## Enrichment Activities
### Plant Glasses
Wrap some artificial flowers or leaves around the frames of a pair of sunglasses or eyeglasses. Invite the children to wear the decorative glasses when reading the word cards posted at the center.

### Gifts From Plants and Trees
Label a box as follows: "Gifts From Plants and Trees." Gather an assortment of objects that come from plants and trees. Place them in the box for the children to explore. As a group, make a list of the items that come from plants and trees. Encourage the children to bring in objects from home to add to the box.

### Plant and Tree Walk
Take the children on a plant and tree walk in your neighborhood. Take photographs of the children next to a variety of plants and trees. Have the pictures developed. Paste them into a blank book or photo album along with a related caption for each picture.

## Suggested Prayer
Thank you, Heavenly Father, for giving us so many different kinds of plants and trees. We think it's great how you spoke the words and created all the different plants and trees for us. Help us to be thankful for their beauty and for all the gifts we receive from them. Guide us in caring for what you have created. We praise you for your works. It's in his name that we pray. Amen.

Name _____

# Where Does It Grow?

Color, cut, and paste.

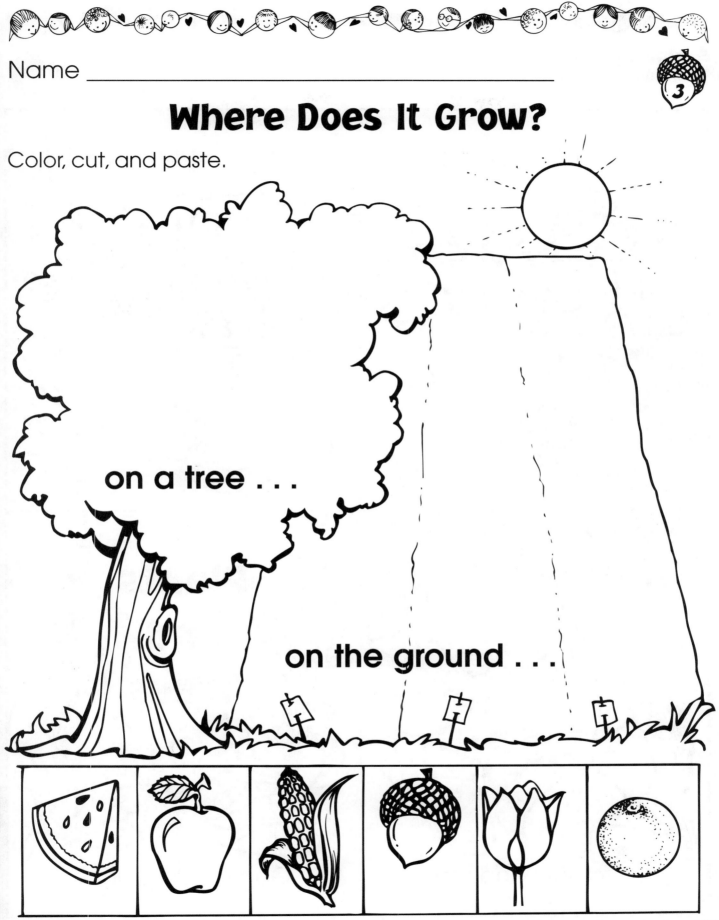

on a tree . . .

on the ground . . .

4

3

He made them all . . .

2

God made trees.

. . . for you and me!

4

**Plants and Trees**

God made plants.

## Activity Cards

Cut apart the cards. Glue them to construction paper. Put them at the center along with any necessary materials.

### Sponge Painting a Tree

**Materials Needed:**
white paper, brown crayon, green paint, sponge pieces, pie plate

**Directions:**
1. Draw a tree trunk using the brown crayon.
2. Dip a sponge piece in green paint.
3. Dab the sponge onto the paper many times to make the top of the tree.
4. Let dry and hang up.

### Plant and Tree Collage

**Materials Needed:**
magazines, scissors, paper, glue

**Directions:**
1. Cut out pictures of plants and trees from magazines.
2. Glue them onto a sheet of paper.
3. Hang the paper on the bulletin board.

### Seed Sort

**Materials Needed:**
collection of seeds

**Directions:**
1. Choose a handful of seeds.
2. Sort the seeds into groups.
3. Tell how you sorted the seeds (size, shape, color, type).
4. Sort the seeds in a different way.

### Measuring Sticks and Branches

**Materials Needed:**
ruler or measuring tape, sticks of different lengths, paper, pencil

**Directions:**
1. Choose 3 or 4 sticks of different lengths.
2. Draw a picture of each stick on your paper.
3. Measure each stick.
4. Write how long each stick is.

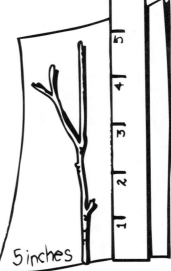

5 inches

## Game

Make two copies of this page and page 7. Color the picture cards. Glue the picture cards to tagboard for durability and cut them out. Store the cards in a resealable bag. Cut out the directions below and place them inside the bag.

### Plant and Tree Memory Game

**Directions:**

1. Randomly lay the cards facedown on a table.
2. Take turns turning over two cards at a time.
3. If you find a match, keep them.
4. Play until all cards have been matched.

Then God said, "Let there be plants and trees."

(Genesis 1:11)

# God Made Me Special

*I praise you because I am fearfully and wonderfully made . . .* (Psalm 139:14)

Children will learn about how special they are in God's eyes as they participate in these Scripture-based learning center activities.

### More From the Bible About How God Made Each of Us Special

Psalm 139:13–16, Jeremiah 32:38, Ezekiel 36:26–27, 1 Corinthians 6:19, Psalm 100:3

## Things to Include at the Center

- copies of Activity Pages 3–4
- Activity Cards (page 5) and any materials needed to complete the activities
- prepared Five Senses Bingo Game (pages 6–7)
- copies of the Shape Journal Page (page 8)
- copies of the Bible Verse Poster (page 9); include one on display
- assortment of art supplies
- children's literature selections relating to children and how each of us is special
- an assortment of children's clothing items for sorting
- assortment of dolls for comparing likenesses and differences
- poster of the human body or skeletal system
- wall growth chart children can use to measure their heights
- bath scale children can use to measure their weights
- measuring tapes children can use to measure various body parts
- five senses box containing items for smelling, tasting, touching, hearing, and seeing
- assortment of pictures and photographs of children from different cultures and nationalities
- photographs of all the children in the class; baby pictures of all the children in the class
- one name card for each child in the class

## Word List

Print the following vocabulary words on 3" x 5" note cards and post them around the center: *me, I am, special, skin, hair, heart, body, eyes, legs, arms, inches, tall, weigh, pounds.* Children can refer to the word cards when writing or reading at the center.

## Directions

1. Discuss the key Bible verse featured above (and the condensed version on the poster page).
2. Go over each activity on pages 3–9 with the children. Demonstrate how to complete each activity from start to finish.
3. Invite the children to explore with the materials at the center and discuss their findings with each other.

## Sentence Starters

Print some of the sentence starters below on a piece of chart paper or directly onto copies of the Shape Journal Page (page 8) for fun writing activities.

I am special because _____.

I'm good at _____.

God made me different from _____.

I am wonderfully made because _____.

I'm special to God because _____.

## For More Fun

Trace around each child's body on butcher paper or mural paper. Invite the children to color or paint clothing, facial features, and hair onto their body shapes. Have the children cut out their body shapes. Hang them around the learning center for an eye-catching display.

## Enrichment Activities

### Handprint Wreath

Pour two or more colors of tempera paints into shallow pans. Invite each child to dip one of his or her hands into the paint and then make a print in a circle formation on a large sheet of mural paper, forming a wreath. Print the key verse (Psalm 139:14) inside the wreath. Have each child sign his or her name near his or her handprint. Hang the wreath in the classroom to remind the children how God made each of them special.

### Me Box

Invite each child to prepare a "Me Box" to bring to class. Have the children work with a family member at home to decorate the outside of a box and then fill it with items that tell about the child (photographs, favorite toys, hobby materials, etc.). Have each child present his or her "Me Box" to the class. Children will enjoy learning about each other and how God made everyone different and special.

### Resource Person

Invite a medical doctor to come in and make a short presentation to the children on how the human body works and what it is made of (i.e., number of bones we have, how the heart pumps blood, etc.). Afterwards, have the children draw a picture of the human body. Then pray a class prayer of thanksgiving to God for creating the human body (see below).

### People Puppets

Provide the children with brown lunch bags, glue, crayons, and an assortment of decorative materials, such as yarn, rickrack, fabric scraps, cotton balls, tissue paper, etc. Have each child design a people puppet. Once the puppets are complete, have pairs of children practice and perform short dialogues about how wonderfully each of us is made.

### Suggested Prayer

Dear God, thank you for making each of us special. We praise you for creating us and knitting us together. Thank you for making our bodies so that we can walk and run and sing and play and work and pray. Help us to use our bodies to glorify you. Amen.

# God Made Us Special

Use crayons to add hair and facial features to each child. Color the clothing on each child. Make each child different.

*Emergent Reader*
Draw a picture in each box. Finish each sentence. Color, cut, fold, and read.

4

**3**

God made my ——————.
I am wonderfully made.

**2**

God gave me ——————.
I am wonderfully made.

# I am
# Wonderfully
# Made

by _____

I'm good at _____.
I am wonderfully made.

**4**

## Activity Cards

Cut apart the cards. Glue them to construction paper. Put them at the center along with any necessary materials.

### Measure and Weigh

**Materials Needed:**
bath scale, wall growth chart, measuring tapes, rulers, paper, pencil

**Directions:**

1. Stand on the bath scale.

2. See how much you weigh and write it down.

3. Stand next to the growth chart.

4. Have a friend read how tall you are. Write it down.

5. Use the measuring tape or ruler to measure other parts of your body: wrist, waist, ankle, arm, leg, etc. Write these measurements down.

### Body Letters

**Materials Needed:**
alphabet poster

**Directions:**

1. Look at the alphabet poster.

2. Choose a letter.

3. Make that letter with your body.

4. Make more letters with your body.

5. Find one or two friends and make a letter together.

### A Book About Me

**Materials Needed:**
blank books, markers or crayons

**Directions:**

1. Draw a picture of yourself on the cover of the book.

2. Write your name on the cover of the book.

3. Draw pictures that tell about you on the pages of the book.

4. Dictate some words to an adult and have him or her write inside your book.

5. Read the book with someone else.

### Self Portrait

**Materials Needed:**
mirror, paints, paintbrushes, sheets of drawing paper entitled "I'm Glad God Made Me"

**Directions:**

1. Look at yourself in the mirror.

2. Paint a picture of yourself.

3. When the picture is dry, hang it up at the learning center.

## Game

Color the three bingo cards on page 7. Mount them on tagboard and laminate them. Cut them apart. Color the picture cards (five senses cards) below. Mount them on tagboard, laminate them, and cut them apart to make three bingo cards. Place the materials, the directions card, and a collection of pennies in a shoebox. Three or four children can play, with the fourth child being the one who draws the cards. As you introduce this game to the children, talk about how God has blessed us with our five senses.

6

### Five Senses Bingo

**Directions:**

1. Stack the five senses cards facedown.
2. Each of two or three players chooses a bingo card and 8 pennies.
3. One child turns over one five senses card at a time and names the picture.
4. If a child has that picture on his or her card, the child must tell which of the five senses the picture shows. The child covers the picture with a penny. (Note: Some pictures may involve several senses. Only one needs to be mentioned.)
5. The player who fills his or her card first with 8 pennies calls out "Bingo! God gave me five senses!"

God made me wonderful!
(Psalm 139:14)